EXPAND YOUR KNITTING SKILLS

MW01041413

Take your basic knitting skills to the next level! Seventeen stylish patterns help you learn these exciting and useful techniques—creating cables, knitting in the round, making thumb gussets for mittens, picking up stitches, and knitting on the diagonal. Whether you choose a hat, scarf, mittens, purse, or hand warmers, you'll be pleasantly surprised at how fast you'll finish your project!

MEET KIM HAESEMEYER

For Kim Haesemeyer, knitting is like breathing—natural and easy. However, she says it wasn't always that way. "My mom taught me to knit when I was young, but my stitches were so tight I broke a needle. Out of frustration, I didn't touch anything knitting-related until after my third child was born, when I taught myself from a kit I purchased on clearance. I started designing because I knew there had to be an easier way to make the projects I wanted. My goal with each design is to create clear patterns that are easy to read and understand, because knitting time is too precious to be spent agonizing over directions."

Kim has designed for yarn manufacturers, and several of her patterns have appeared in popular knitting magazines.

To catch up with Kim, visit her blog at BigSkyYarnsAndCrafts.com, and see more of her designs at Ravelry.com, where her user name is KimH.

LEISURE ARTS, INC.
Little Rock, Arkansas

TABLE OF CONTENTS

STARTER CABLE SCARF & HAT

If you haven't knit cables before, this is a terrific set to get you started. Since the cable row is worked only every 10 rows and the pattern uses bulky yarn, you'll have this hat and scarf finished in no time. The scarf is truly easy because it is worked flat. The hat is considered an intermediate project, because it is knit in the round. However, it has no seams to stitch! Chances are excellent that you're going to fall in love with knitting cables!

MATERIALS

BULKY 5

Bulky Weight Yarn
[5 ounces, 153 yards
(140 grams, 140 meters) per skein]:
    Scarf: 2 skeins
    Hat (all sizes): 1 skein
Knitting needles **(use size needed for gauge)**
    Scarf: Straight needles, size 11 (8 mm)
    Hat: 16" (40.5 cm) Circular needle,
        size 11 (8 mm) (for Brim & Body) **and**
        a set of 4 double-pointed needles,
        size 11 (8 mm) (for Shaping)
Cable needle
Split-ring marker for Hat
Yarn needle

STITCH GUIDE

Cables are achieved with a simple twisting, by exchanging the position of your stitches. The most common cables are formed by slipping part of the cable stitches "on-hold" onto a cable needle, then holding the stitches either in the "front" or in the "back" of your work. Stitches are worked from the left needle, then you work the "on-hold" stitches, either by working them directly from the cable needle **or** by slipping them back onto the left needle and working them.

CABLE 8 BACK (*abbreviated C8B*)

With yarn at the **back** of work, slip the next 4 sts **purlwise** (*Fig.1a*) onto the cable needle. Holding the cable needle at the **back** of work (*Fig.1b*), knit the next 4 sts on the left needle (*Fig. 1c*), then knit the 4 sts on the cable needle (*Fig. 1d*).

Fig. 1a

Fig. 1b

Fig. 1c

Fig. 1d

BORDER

With straight knitting needles, cast on 18 sts.

Row 1: P3, K2, P2, (K1, P2) twice, K2, P3.

Row 2 (Right side): K3, P2, K2, (P1, K2) twice, P2, K3.

Rows 3-9: Repeat Rows 1 and 2, 3 times; then repeat Row 1 once **more**.

BODY

Row 1 (Right side - Cable row): K3, P2, C8B, P2, K3.

Row 2: P3, K2, P8, K2, P3.

Row 3: K3, P2, K8, P2, K3.

Rows 4-10: Repeat Rows 2 and 3, 3 times; then repeat Row 2 once **more**.

Repeat Rows 1-10 for pattern until Scarf measures approximately 58" (147.5 cm) from cast on edge, ending by working Row 10.

BORDER

Row 1 (Right side - Cable row): K3, P2, C8B, P2, K3.

Row 2: P3, K2, P2, (K1, P2) twice, K2, P3.

Row 3: K3, P2, K2, (P1, K2) twice, P2, K3.

Rows 4-9: Repeat Rows 2 and 3, 3 times.

Bind off all sts **loosely** in pattern.

SCARF

◼◼◻◻ EASY

Finished Size:
  3¹/₂" wide x 60" long (9 cm x 152.5 cm)

GAUGE: In Body pattern, 18 sts = 3¹/₂" (9 cm)

HAT

◼◼◼◻ INTERMEDIATE

Size	Fits Head Circumference
Baby	13-15" (33-38 cm)
Child	16-19" (40.5-48.5 cm)
Adult	20-23" (51-58.5 cm)

Finished Circumference:
13¾{16½-19¼}"/35{42-49} cm
Finished Length: 6{7-7½}"/15{18-19} cm

Size Note: Instructions are written for Baby size with Child and Adult sizes in braces { }. Instructions will be easier to read if you circle all the numbers pertaining to the size you're making. If only one number is given, it applies to all sizes.

GAUGE: In Body pattern,
14 sts (one repeat) = 2¾" (7 cm)

Techniques used:
K2 tog *(Fig. 7, page 42)*
P2 tog *(Fig. 8, page 42)*
SSK *(Figs. 9a-c, page 42)*

BRIM
With circular knitting needle *(see Circular Knitting & Using A Circular Needle, page 41)*, cast on 70{84-98} sts; place marker to indicate the beginning of the round *(see Markers, page 40)*.

Rnd 1 (Right side): ★ K2, P2, K2, (P1, K2) twice, P2; repeat from ★ around.

Repeat Rnd 1 for pattern until Brim measures approximately ½{1½-2}"/1.5{4-5} cm from cast on edge.

BODY
Rnd 1 (Right side - Cable rnd): (K2, P2, C8B, P2) around.

Rnds 2-10: (K2, P2, K8, P2) around.

Rnd 11 (Cable rnd): (K2, P2, C8B, P2) around.

SHAPING
Note: Begin knitting with the double-pointed knitting needles when the stitches will not slide easily around the circular knitting needle.

Rnd 1: (K2, P2 tog, K8, P2 tog) around: 60{72-84} sts.

Rnd 2: (K2, P1, K8, P1) around.

Rnd 3: (K2, P1, SSK, K4, K2 tog, P1) around: 50{60-70} sts.

Rnd 4: (K2, P1, K6, P1) around.

Rnd 5: (K2, P1, SSK, K2, K2 tog, P1) around: 40{48-56} sts.

Rnd 6: (K2, P1, K4, P1) around.

Rnd 7: (K2, P1, SSK, K2 tog, P1) around: 30{36-42} sts.

Rnd 8: (K2, P1) around.

Rnd 9: (K2, P1, K2 tog, P1) around: 25{30-35} sts.

Rnd 10: (K2, P1, K1, P1) around.

Rnd 11: (K2, K2 tog, P1) around: 20{24-28} sts.

Rnd 12: (K2, P2 tog) around: 15{18-21} sts.

Rnd 13: (K2 tog, P1) around: 10{12-14} sts.

Cut yarn, leaving a long end for sewing.

Thread the yarn needle with the long end. Slip the remaining sts onto the yarn needle, then onto the long end; gather **tightly** to close the opening, then secure the end.

LUCKY HORSESHOE HAND WARMERS

You'll have good luck making this unique cable! It is actually two cables, one twisted to the front and one to the back, creating the horseshoe effect. The body of these hand warmers is simple K2, P2 ribbing that stretches to fit a wide range of sizes. Finishing is as simple as seaming the sides together while leaving a thumb hole on one side.

 EASY

Size: One size fits most
Fits Hand Circumference: 7 to 10" (18 to 25.5 cm)
Finished Hand Circumference (unstretched):
  6" (15 cm)

MATERIALS
Super Fine Weight Yarn
[3.5 ounces, 437 yards
(100 grams, 400 meters) per hank]:
  1 hank
Straight knitting needles, size 2 (2.75 mm) **or
  size needed for gauge**
Cable needle
Tapestry needle

GAUGE: In K2, P2 ribbing (unstretched),
       52 sts and 40 rows = 4" (10 cm)

STITCH GUIDE
Cables are achieved with a simple twisting, by exchanging the position of your stitches. The most common cables are formed by slipping part of the cable stitches "on-hold" onto a cable needle, then holding the stitches either in the "front" or in the "back" of your work. Stitches are worked from the left needle, then you work the "on-hold" stitches, either by working them directly from the cable needle **or** by slipping them back onto the left needle and working them.

CABLE 10 BACK *(abbreviated C10B)*
With yarn at the **back** of work, slip the next 5 sts **purlwise** onto the cable needle. Holding the cable needle at the **back** of the work, knit the next 5 sts on the left needle, then knit the 5 sts on the cable needle *(Figs. 1a-d, page 2)*.

CABLE 10 FRONT *(abbreviated C10F)*
With yarn at the **back** of work, slip the next 5 sts **purlwise** onto the cable needle. Holding the cable needle at the **front** of the work, knit the next 5 sts on the left needle, then knit the 5 sts on the cable needle.

HAND WARMER (Make 2)
TOP PANEL
WRIST RIBBING
Cast on 42 sts.

Row 1: P2, (K2, P2) across.

Row 2 (Right side): K2, (P2, K2) across.

Repeat Rows 1 and 2 for pattern until Wrist Ribbing measures approximately 2½" (6.5 cm), ending by working Row 1.

BODY

Row 1 (Right side): K2, P2, K2, P5, K 20, P5, K2, P2, K2.

Row 2: P2, K2, P2, K5, P 20, K5, P2, K2, P2.

Row 3 (Cable row)**:** K2, P2, K2, P5, C10B, C10F, P5, K2, P2, K2.

Row 4: P2, K2, P2, K5, P 20, K5, P2, K2, P2.

Row 5: K2, P2, K2, P5, K 20, P5, K2, P2, K2.

Row 6: P2, K2, P2, K5, P 20, K5, P2, K2, P2.

Rows 7-14: Repeat Rows 5 and 6, 4 times.

Rows 15-56: Repeat Rows 3-14, 3 times; then repeat Rows 3-8 once **more**.

FINGER RIBBING

Row 1 (Right side): K2, (P2, K2) across.

Row 2: P2, (K2, P2) across.

Repeat Rows 1 and 2 for pattern until Finger Ribbing measures approximately 1¹/₂" (4 cm), ending by working Row 2.

Bind off all sts in pattern.

BOTTOM PANEL

Cast on 38 sts.

Row 1: P2, (K2, P2) across.

Row 2 (Right side): K2, (P2, K2) across.

Repeat Rows 1 and 2 for pattern until Bottom Panel measures same as Top Panel, ending by working Row 1.

Bind off all sts in pattern.

FINISHING

Weave the seam completely down one side of one Hand Warmer *(Fig. 12, page 43)*; then weave the seam completely down the opposite side of the second Hand Warmer.

On the remaining open edge, weave a 2" (5 cm) seam down from the top edge of the Finger Ribbing; then weave the seam up from the bottom edge of the Wrist Ribbing, leaving a 2¹/₂" (6.5 cm) opening for the thumb.

Repeat on the second Hand Warmer.

THREE-CABLE HAND WARMERS

Three identical cables line up nicely on the backs of these hand warmers. Although the cables are just alike, if you look closely at any one of the cables, you'll see that its two curves are not mirror-image. Instead, they are slightly uneven, an interesting effect that is easily achieved by the addition of a purl stitch.

Shown on page 12.

◼◼◻◻ **EASY**

Sizes: Medium/Large {X-Large}
Fits Hand Circumference:
  7-8{9-10}"/18-20.5{23-25.5} cm
Finished Hand Circumference (unstretched):
  6¼{7¼}"/16{18.5} cm

Size Note: Instructions are written for Medium/Large size with X-Large size in braces { }. Instructions will be easier to read if you circle all the numbers pertaining to the size you're making. If only one number is given, it applies to both sizes.

MATERIALS

Medium Weight Yarn **(4)** MEDIUM
[3 ounces, 132 yards
(85 grams, 121 meters) per skein]:
  1 skein
Straight knitting needles, size 8 (5 mm) **or**
  size needed for gauge
Cable needle
Yarn needle

GAUGE: In K2, P1 ribbing (unstretched),
    23 sts and 26 rows = 4" (10 cm)

STITCH GUIDE

Cables are achieved with a simple twisting, by exchanging the position of your stitches. The most common cables are formed by slipping part of the cable stitches "on-hold" onto a cable needle, then holding the stitches either in the "front" or in the "back" of your work. Stitches are worked from the left needle, then you work the "on-hold" stitches, either by working them directly from the cable needle **or** by slipping them back onto the left needle and working them.

CABLE 5 BACK *(abbreviated C5B)*
With yarn at the **back** of work, slip the next 3 sts **purlwise** onto the cable needle. Holding the cable needle at the **back** of the work, knit the next 2 sts on the left needle, then (P1, K2) from the cable needle *(Figs. 1a-d, page 2)*.

HAND WARMER (Make 2)
TOP PANEL
WRIST RIBBING
Cast on 23 sts.

Row 1: P2, (K1, P2) across.

Row 2 (Right side): K2, (P1, K2) across.

Repeat Rows 1 and 2 for pattern until Wrist Ribbing measures approximately 2½" (6.5 cm) from cast on edge, ending by working Row 1.

BODY

Row 1 (Right side - Cable row): K2, P1, (C5B, P1) across to last 2 sts, K2.

Row 2: P2, (K1, P2) across.

Row 3: K2, (P1, K2) across.

Row 4: P2, (K1, P2) across.

Rows 5 and 6: Repeat Rows 3 and 4.

Row 7 (Cable row): K2, P1, (C5B, P1) across to last 2 sts, K2.

Rows 8-19: Repeat Rows 2-7 twice.

FINGER RIBBING

Row 1: P2, (K1, P2) across.

Row 2 (Right side): K2, (P1, K2) across.

Repeat Rows 1 and 2 for pattern until Finger Ribbing measures approximately 1½" (4 cm), ending by working Row 1.

Bind off all sts in pattern.

BOTTOM PANEL

Cast on 17{23} sts.

Row 1: P2, (K1, P2) across.

Row 2 (Right side): K2, (P1, K2) across.

Repeat Rows 1 and 2 for pattern until Bottom Panel measures same as Top Panel, ending by working Row 1.

Bind off all sts in pattern.

FINISHING

Weave the seam completely down one side of one Hand Warmer *(Fig. 12, page 43)*; then weave the seam completely down the opposite side of the second Hand Warmer.

On the remaining open edge, weave a 1½" (4 cm) seam down from the top edge of the Finger Ribbing; then weave the seam up from the bottom edge of the Wrist Ribbing, leaving a 2½" (6.5 cm) opening for the thumb.

Repeat on the second Hand Warmer.

COLOR-CHANGING SCARF

You'll master three fun techniques with this one striking scarf—changing yarn colors, knitting on the diagonal, and working with two strands of yarn.

 EASY

Finished Size:
  4¹/₂" wide x 71" long (11.5 cm x 180.5 cm)

MATERIALS

Medium Weight Yarn **(4 MEDIUM)**
[3.5 ounces, 220 yards
(100 grams, 201 meters) per hank]:
  Light Color (L) - 1 hank
  Medium Color (M) - 1 hank
  Dark Color (D) - 1 hank
Straight knitting needles, size 10¹/₂ (6.5 mm) **or size needed for gauge**
Split-ring marker (optional)
Yarn needle

Note: Scarf is made holding 2 strands of yarn together throughout.

GAUGE: With 2 strands of yarn held together, in Garter Stitch (knit every row), 12 sts and 16 rows = 4" (10 cm)

Techniques used:
K2 tog *(Fig. 7, page 42)*
YO *(Fig. 10, page 43)*

SCARF
INCREASING TRIANGLE

With 2 strands of Dark Color (DD) held together, cast on 2 sts.

Rows 1 and 2: Knit across.

Row 3: K1, YO, K1: 3 sts.

Row 4: K2, YO, K1: 4 sts.

Row 5: K2, YO, knit across: 5 sts.

Repeat Row 5 with DD until 20 sts are on the needles **or** approximately 5" (12.5 cm), measuring from bottom right corner straight up along side edge, **not** measuring on the diagonal.

Cut one strand of Dark Color (D) leaving a 6" (15 cm) length to weave in later. With Medium Color (M), tie a temporary knot around remaining Dark Color (D) strand, having knot close to needle.

BODY

With one strand **each** of Medium Color and Dark Color (MD) held together, continue as follows:

Row 1 (Right side): K2, YO, knit across: 21 sts.

Row 2: K1, K2 tog, YO, K2 tog, knit across: 20 sts.

Following Color Chart, page 14, repeat Rows 1 and 2 until each color section measures amount indicated on chart, switching colors in same manner for next color section ONLY at the beginning of Row 1.

DECREASING TRIANGLE

Row 1 (Right side): With DD, K1, K2 tog, YO, K2 tog, knit across: 19 sts.

Rows 2-14: K1, K2 tog, YO, K2 tog, knit across: 6 sts.

Row 15: K1, K2 tog, YO, K3: 6 sts.

Row 16: K1, K2 tog twice, K1: 4 sts.

Row 17: K2 tog twice: 2 sts.

Cut yarn, leaving a long end for sewing.

Thread the yarn needle with the long end.
Slip the remaining 2 sts onto the yarn needle, then onto the long end. Secure the end by weaving it in on the wrong side of the Scarf.

COLOR CHART

Work entire Color Chart, measuring each color section straight up along the side edge, ending each section by working Row 2.

MD	3"	(7.5 cm)
MM	3"	(7.5 cm)
LM	3"	(7.5 cm)
LL	11"	(28 cm)
LM	3"	(7.5 cm)
MM	3"	(7.5 cm)
MD	4"	(10 cm)
DD	8"	(20.5 cm)
MD	4"	(10 cm)
MM	3"	(7.5 cm)
LM	3"	(7.5 cm)
LL	10"	(25.5 cm)
LM	3"	(7.5 cm)
MM	2½"	(6.5 cm)
MD	2½"	(6.5 cm)

KEY
LL = 2 strands Light Color
LM = 1 strand **each** Light Color & Medium Color
MM = 2 strands Medium Color
MD = 1 strand **each** Medium Color & Dark Color
DD = 2 strands Dark Color

CLASSIC RIBBED SCARF & HAT

The K4, P4 ribbing of this set is simple to do while yielding an attractive fabric. The scarf is a breeze, worked flat and quickly. The hat uses both circular and double-pointed needles, which is much easier than you may think. Refer to Circular Knitting in the General Instructions to learn the basics of using these tools for knitting-in-the-round. You'll be pleased at the excellent results you'll achieve with these standard knitting techniques!

Shown on page 17.

MATERIALS

Medium Weight Yarn **[MEDIUM 4]**
[3.5 ounces, 132 yards
(100 grams, 121 meters) per hank]:
  Scarf: 2 hanks
  Hat (all sizes): 1 hank
Knitting needles **(use size needed for gauge)**
  Scarf: Straight needles, size 10½ (6.5 mm)
  Hat: 16" (40.5 cm) Circular needle (for Brim & Body) **and** a set of 4 double-pointed needles, size 10 (6 mm) (for Shaping)
Split-ring marker for Hat
Yarn needle

SCARF

■□□ EASY

Finished Size (unstretched):
  3½" wide x 50" long (9 cm x 127 cm)

GAUGE: In K4, P4 ribbing (unstretched),
       24 sts = 3½" (9 cm)

BODY

With straight knitting needles, cast on 24 sts.

Row 1: (K4, P4) across.

Repeat Row 1 for ribbing until Scarf measures approximately 50" (127 cm) from cast on edge.

Bind off all sts **loosely** in **ribbing**.

HAT

■■■□ INTERMEDIATE

Size	Fits Head Circumference
Baby/Toddler	15-17" (38-43 cm)
Child Medium	17-19" (43-48.5 cm)
Adult Medium	19-21" (48.5-53.5 cm)
Adult Large	21-23" (53.5-58.5 cm)

Finished Circumference (slightly stretched):
  14{15¾-17½-19¼}"/35.5{40-44.5-49} cm
Finished Length (with Brim turned up):
  6{7-8-8}"/15{18-20.5-20.5} cm

Size Note: Instructions are written for Baby/Toddler size with Child Medium, Adult Medium, and Adult Large sizes in braces { }. Instructions will be easier to read if you circle all the numbers pertaining to the size you're making. If only one number is given, it applies to all sizes.

GAUGE: In K4, P4 ribbing (slightly stretched),
       16 sts and 18 rnds = 3½" (9 cm)

Techniques used:
K2 tog *(Fig. 7, page 42)*
P2 tog *(Fig. 8, page 42)*

BRIM

With circular knitting needle *(see Circular Knitting & Using A Circular Needle, page 41)*, cast on 64{72-80-88} sts; place marker to indicate the beginning of the round *(see Markers, page 40)*.

Rnd 1: (K4, P4) around.

Repeat Rnd 1 for ribbing until Brim measures approximately 2{2-2½-2½}"/5{5-6.5-6.5} cm from cast on edge.

BODY

Rnd 1 (Right side): (P4, K4) around.

Repeat Rnd 1 for ribbing until Hat measures approximately 5¾{6¾-8¼-8¼}"/14.5{17-21-21} cm from cast on edge.

SHAPING

Note: Begin knitting with the double-pointed knitting needles when the stitches will not slide easily around the circular knitting needle.

Rnd 1: (P2 tog, P2, K4) around: 56{63-70-77} sts.

Rnd 2: (P3, K4) around.

Rnd 3: (P2 tog, P1, K4) around: 48{54-60-66} sts.

Rnd 4: (P2, K4) around.

Rnd 5: (P2 tog, K4) around: 40{45-50-55} sts.

Rnd 6: (P1, K4) around.

Rnd 7: (P1, K2 tog, K2) around: 32{36-40-44} sts.

Rnd 8: (P1, K3) around.

Rnd 9: (P1, K2 tog, K1) around: 24{27-30-33} sts.

Rnd 10: (P1, K2 tog) around: 16{18-20-22} sts.

Rnd 11: K2 tog around: 8{9-10-11} sts.

Cut yarn, leaving a long end for sewing.

Thread the yarn needle with the long end. Slip the remaining sts onto the yarn needle, then onto the long end; gather **tightly** to close the opening, then secure the end.

IMPRESSIVE SCARF & HAT

If you can make knit and purl stitches, you can create this textured set! The Broken Rib pattern stitch makes the fabric look more complex than it is. Even better, the bulky yarn makes these toasty accessories finish quickly! The hat is worked flat on straight needles, with the side seams sewn together and the top edge gathered to finish. The scarf is also worked flat, but on circular needles to hold more stitches.

MATERIALS

SUPER BULKY (6)

Super Bulky Weight Yarn
[6 ounces, 106 yards
(170 grams, 97 meters) per skein]:
  Scarf: 2 skeins
  Hat (both sizes): 1 skein
Knitting needles **(use size needed for gauge)**
  Scarf: 24" (61 cm) Circular needle,
    size 13 (9 mm)
  Hat: Straight needles, size 13 (9 mm)
Yarn needle

SCARF

◼◼◻◻◻ EASY

Finished Size (slightly stretched):
  3¹/₂" wide x 48¹/₂{59¹/₂}" long
  9 cm x 123{151} cm

Size Note: Instructions are written for Child size with Adult size in braces { }. Instructions will be easier to read if you circle all the numbers pertaining to the size you're making. If only one number is given, it applies to both sizes.

GAUGE: In pattern (slightly stretched),
        10 sts and 13 rows = 4" (10 cm)

BODY

With circular knitting needle, cast on 121{149} sts; work back and forth in rows on the circular needle (do **not** join sts).

Row 1: (K3, P1) across to last st, K1.

Repeat Row 1 for pattern until Scarf measures approximately 3¹/₂" (9 cm) from cast on edge.

Bind off all sts **loosely** in pattern.

HAT

◼◼◼◻◻ INTERMEDIATE

Size	Fits Head Circumference
Baby/Toddler	16-17" (40.5-43 cm)
Child	18-19" (45.5-48.5 cm)
Adult Medium	20-21" (51-53.5 cm)
Adult Large	22-23" (56-58.5 cm)

Finished Circumference (unstretched):
  16{17¹/₂-19¹/₄-20³/₄}"/40.5{44.5-49-52.5} cm
Finished Length:
  6¹/₂{7-7¹/₂-8}"/16.5{18-19-20.5} cm

Size Note: Instructions are written for Baby/Toddler size with Child, Adult Medium, and Adult Large sizes in braces { }. Instructions will be easier to read if you circle all the numbers pertaining to the size you're making. If only one number is given, it applies to all sizes.

GAUGE: In pattern (unstretched),
        10 sts and 13 rows = 4" (10 cm)

Techniques used:
K2 tog *(Fig. 7, page 42)*
P2 tog *(Fig. 8, page 42)*

BODY

With straight knitting needles,
cast on 42{46-50-54} sts.

Row 1: (P1, K3) across to last 2 sts, P2.

Row 2 (Right side): (K3, P1) across to last 2 sts, K2.

Repeat Rows 1 and 2 for pattern until Body
measures approximately 4³/₄{5¹/₄-5³/₄-6¹/₄}"/
12{13.5-14.5-16} cm from cast on edge, ending
by working Row 1.

SHAPING

Row 1 (Right side): K2, (P2 tog, P1, K1) across:
32{35-38-41} sts.

Row 2: (P1, K2) across to last 2 sts, P2.

Row 3: K2, (P2 tog, K1) across: 22{24-26-28} sts.

Row 4: (P1, K1) across to last 2 sts, P2.

Row 5: K2 tog across: 11{12-13-14} sts.

Row 6: P2 tog across to last 1{0-1-0} st(s) *(see
Zeros, page 40)*, P1{0-1-0}: 6{6-7-7} sts.

Cut yarn, leaving a long end for sewing.

Thread the yarn needle with the long end.
Slip the remaining sts onto the yarn needle, then
onto the long end. Gather **tightly** to close the
opening, then weave the seam *(Fig. 12, page 43)*.

LONG SPIRAL SCARF & SIMPLE HAT

This scarf gets its swirling shape from adding yarn overs every fourth row—it's just that easy! Never knitted in the round before? Here's a hat that's tops for learning how! Self-striping yarn brightens the Stockinette Stitch fabric on both pieces.

Shown on page 26.

MATERIALS
Medium Weight Yarn 【4】
[1.75 ounces, 98 yards
(50 grams, 90 meters) per ball]:
  Scarf: 2 skeins
  Hat (all sizes): 1{1-1-2} skein(s)
Knitting needles **(use size needed for gauge)**
  Scarf: Two 29" (73.5 cm) Circular needles,
    size 11 (8 mm)
  Hat - Baby & Child Sizes ONLY:
    Set of 4 double-pointed needles,
    sizes 9 (5.5 mm) **and** 11 (8 mm)
  Hat - Adult Medium & Large Sizes ONLY:
    16" (40.5 cm) Circular needles, sizes 9
    (5.5 mm) **and** 11 (8 mm) (for Brim & Body)
    and a set of 4 double-pointed needles,
    size 11 (8 mm) (for Shaping)
Markers for Hat: Color A (split-ring) - 1;
  Color B - 4{5-6-7}
Yarn needle

SCARF
◼◼◻◻ **EASY**

Finished Size: 2¼" wide x 48" long
(measured along cast on edge) (5.5 cm x 122 cm)

GAUGE: In Stockinette Stitch
      (knit one row, purl one row),
      15 sts and 20 rows = 4" (10 cm)

Technique used:
YO *(Fig. 10, page 43)*

Note: Two circular knitting needles are necessary to accommodate the large number of sts. Knit back and forth in rows as if you were using straight needles (do **not** join sts). Place rubber bands or point protectors on one end of each needle to keep the sts from slipping off.

BODY
With circular knitting needle, cast on 80 sts.

Row 1: Purl across.

Row 2 (Right side - Increase row): K1, (YO, K1) across: 159 sts.

Row 3: Purl across.

Row 4: Knit across.

Row 5: Purl across.

Rows 6-13: Repeat Rows 2-5 twice: 633 sts.

Bind off all sts **loosely** in **knit.**

HAT

Size	Fits Head Circumference
Baby	14-16" (35.5-40.5 cm)
Child	17-19" (43-48.5 cm)
Adult Medium	20-22" (51-56 cm)
Adult Large	23-24" (58.5-61 cm)

Finished Circumference (unstretched):
13$\frac{1}{4}${16-18$\frac{3}{4}$-21$\frac{1}{4}$}"/33.5{40.5-47.5-54} cm
Finished Length (unrolled):
7{7$\frac{1}{2}$-8$\frac{1}{2}$-9}"/18{19-21.5-23} cm

Size Note: Instructions are written for Baby size with Child, Adult Medium, and Adult Large sizes in braces { }. Instructions will be easier to read if you circle all the numbers pertaining to the size you're making. If only one number is given, it applies to all sizes.

GAUGE: With larger size needle(s),
in Stockinette Stitch (knit every rnd),
15 sts and 20 rnds = 4" (10 cm)

Techniques used:
K2 tog *(Fig. 7, page 42)*
P2 tog *(Fig. 8, page 42)*

BRIM

For Baby & Child Sizes ONLY: With larger size knitting needles, cast on 50{60} sts; divide sts between 3 double-pointed needles *(see Circular Knitting & Using Double-Pointed Needles, page 41)*. Place Color A marker around the first stitch to indicate the beginning of the round *(see Markers, page 40)*.

For Adult Medium & Large Sizes ONLY: With larger size circular knitting needle *(see Circular Knitting & Using A Circular Needle, page 41)*, cast on {70-80} sts; place Color A marker to indicate the beginning of the round *(see Markers, page 40)*.

ALL Sizes - Rnds 1-5 (Right side): Knit around.

BODY
Change to smaller size needle(s).

Rnds 1-5: Knit around.

Change back to larger size needle(s) and knit around until Hat measures approximately 5{5$\frac{1}{2}$-6$\frac{1}{2}$-7}"/12.5{14-16.5-18} cm from cast on edge.

SHAPING
Note for Adult Medium & Large Sizes: Begin knitting with the double-pointed knitting needles when the stitches will not slide easily around the circular knitting needle.

Rnd 1: K8, K2 tog, (place Color B marker, K8, K2 tog) around: 45{54-63-72} sts.

Rnd 2: Knit around, slipping Color B markers.

Rnd 3: Knit across to within 2 sts of first Color B marker, K2 tog, ★ slip marker, knit across to within 2 sts of next Color B marker, K2 tog; repeat from ★ around to last Color B marker, slip marker, knit across to within 2 sts of Color A marker, K2 tog: 40{48-56-64} sts.

Rnd 4: Knit around, slipping Color B markers.

Rnds 5-10: Knit across to within 2 sts of first Color B marker, K2 tog, ★ slip marker, knit across to within 2 sts of next Color B marker, K2 tog; repeat from ★ around to last Color B marker, slip marker, knit across to within 2 sts of Color A marker, K2 tog: 10{12-14-16} sts.

Cut yarn, leaving a long end for sewing.

Thread the yarn needle with the long end. Slip the remaining sts onto the yarn needle while removing all markers, then onto the long end; gather **tightly** to close the opening, then secure the end.

THREE PIECE GIFT SET

From the stylish "slouch" hat to the warm mittens, this is a gift set any girl (of any age!) would love to wear. Self-striping yarn adds excitement to the simple fabric. The hat and mittens are knit in the round on double-pointed needles, with the additional use of circular needles on the adult sizes, as well as the Child's Medium hat. The hat is seamless and gathered at the top. The short spiral scarf uses two circular needles to easily accommodate the long rows of stitches.

MATERIALS

Medium Weight Yarn 🔵 **4**
[2.8 ounces, 110 yards
(80 grams, 100 meters) per skein]:
  Scarf: 1 skein
  Slouch Hat (all sizes): 2 skeins
  Mittens: {1-1-1}{2-2-2} skein(s)
Knitting needles **(use size needed for gauge)**
  Scarf: Two 24" (61 cm) Circular needles,
    size 10 (6 mm)
  Slouch Hat - Baby/Toddler Size ONLY: Set of
    4 double-pointed needles, sizes 8 (5 mm) **and**
    10 (6 mm)
  Slouch Hat - Child Medium & Adult Size
    ONLY: 16" (40.5 cm) Circular needles,
    sizes 8 (5 mm) **and** 10 (6 mm) (for Brim &
    Body) **and** a set of 4 double-pointed needles,
    size 10 (6 mm) (for Shaping)
  Mittens: Set of 4 double-pointed needles,
    size 10 (6 mm)
Markers:
  Slouch Hat: Color A (split-ring) - 1;
    Color B - 8{9-10}
  Mittens: Color A (split-ring) - 1; Color B - 3
Waste (scrap) yarn for Thumb Gusset of Mittens
Yarn needle

SCARF

⬛⬛⬜⬜ **EASY**

Finished Size: 2½" wide x 27" long
  (measured along cast on edge) (6.5 cm x 68.5 cm)

GAUGE: In Stockinette Stitch
  (knit one row, purl one row),
  18 sts and 24 rows = 4" (10 cm)

Technique used:
YO (*Fig. 10, page 43*)

Note: Two circular knitting needles are necessary to accommodate the large number of sts. Knit back and forth in rows as if you were using straight needles (do **not** join sts). Place rubber bands or point protectors on one end of each needle to keep the sts from slipping off.

BODY

With circular knitting needle, cast on 50 sts.

Row 1: Purl across.

Row 2 (Right side - Increase row): K1, (YO, K1) across: 99 sts.

Row 3: Purl across.

Row 4: Knit across.

Row 5: Purl across.

Rows 6-13: Repeat Rows 2-5 twice: 393 sts.

Bind off all sts **loosely** in **knit**.

HAT

Size	Fits Head Circumference
Baby/Toddler	14-17" (35.5-43 cm)
Child Medium	18-20" (45.5-51 cm)
Adult	21-23" (53.5-58.5 cm)

Finished Circumference (unstretched):
  12{14-16}"/30.5{35.5-40.5} cm
Finished Length (all sizes): 9" (23 cm)

Size Note: Instructions are written for Baby/Toddler size with Child Medium and Adult sizes in braces { }. Instructions will be easier to read if you circle all the numbers pertaining to the size you're making. If only one number is given, it applies to all sizes.

GAUGE: With larger size needle(s),
        in Stockinette Stitch (knit every rnd),
        18 sts and 24 rnds = 4" (10 cm)
        in K2, P2 ribbing,
        24 sts and 24 rnds = 4" (10 cm)

Techniques used:
M1L *(Figs. 5a & b, page 42)*
K2 tog *(Fig. 7, page 42)*

RIBBING

For Baby/Toddler Size ONLY: With smaller size knitting needles, cast on 72 sts; divide sts evenly between 3 double-pointed needles *(see Circular Knitting & Using Double-Pointed Needles, page 41)*. Place Color A marker around the first stitch to indicated the beginning of the round *(see Markers, page 40)*.

For Child Medium & Adult Sizes ONLY: With smaller size circular knitting needle *(see Circular Knitting & Using A Circular Needle, page 41)*, cast on {84-96} sts; place Color A marker to indicate the beginning of the round *(see Markers, page 40)*.

ALL Sizes - Rnd 1 (Right side): (K2, P2) around.

Repeat Rnd 1 until Ribbing measures approximately 1½" (4 cm) from cast on edge.

BODY
Change to larger size needle(s).

Baby/Toddler Size ONLY - Rnd 1: (K2, M1L) around: 108 sts.

Child Medium & Adult Sizes ONLY - Rnd 1:
★ K{2-3}, M1L, K{3-2}, M1L, K{2-3}, M1L; repeat from ★ around: {120-132} sts.

ALL Sizes: Knit every round until Hat measures approximately 5½" (14 cm) from cast on edge **or** 3½" (9 cm) less than desired finished length.

SHAPING
Note for Child Medium & Adult Sizes: Begin knitting with the double-pointed knitting needles when the stitches will not slide easily around the circular knitting needle.

Rnd 1: K 10, K2 tog, (place Color B marker, K 10, K2 tog) around: 99{110-121} sts.

Rnd 2: Knit around, slipping Color B markers.

Rnd 3 (Decrease rnd): Knit across to within 2 sts of first Color B marker, K2 tog, ★ slip marker, knit across to within 2 sts of next Color B marker, K2 tog; repeat from ★ around to last Color B marker, slip marker, knit across to within 2 sts of Color A marker, K2 tog: 90{100-110} sts.

Rnds 4-21: Repeat Rnds 2 and 3, 9 times: 9{10-11} sts.

Cut yarn, leaving a long end for sewing.

Thread the yarn needle with the long end. Slip the remaining sts onto the yarn needle while removing all markers, then onto the long end; gather **tightly** to close the opening, then secure the end.

MITTENS

■■■□ INTERMEDIATE

Size	Finished Mitten Circumference	
Toddler (ages 2-3)	5¼"	(13.5 cm)
Child Small (ages 4-6)	6¼"	(16 cm)
Child Medium (ages 7-10)	7"	(18 cm)
Child Large/Women's Medium	8"	(20.5 cm)
Women's Large/Men's Medium	9"	(23 cm)
Men's Large	9¾"	(25 cm)

Size Note: Instructions are written with Toddler, Child Small, and Child Medium sizes in the first set of braces { } and with Child Large/Women's Medium, Women's Large/Men's Medium, and Men's Large sizes in the second set of braces. Instructions will be easier to read if you circle all the numbers pertaining to the size you're making. If only one number is given, it applies to all sizes.

GAUGE: In Stockinette Stitch (knit every rnd), 18 sts and 24 rnds = 4" (10 cm)

Techniques used:
M1L *(Figs. 5a & b, page 42)*
M1R *(Figs. 6a & b, page 42)*
K2 tog *(Fig. 7, page 42)*

RIGHT MITTEN
CUFF
Cast on {24-24-28}{32-36-40} sts; divide sts onto 3 double-pointed knitting needles *(see Circular Knitting & Using Double-Pointed Needles, page 41)*. Place Color A marker around the first stitch to indicate the beginning of the round *(see Markers, page 40)*.

Rnd 1 (Right side): (K2, P2) across.

Repeat Rnd 1 for K2, P2 ribbing until Cuff measures approximately {2½-2½-3}{3-3½-3½}"/ {6.5-6.5-7.5}{7.5-9-9} cm from cast on edge.

All Sizes EXCEPT Toddler Size - Increase Rnd:
★ Knit {6-7}{8-9-10} sts, M1L; repeat from ★ around: {28-32}{36-40-44} sts.

ALL Sizes - Next 3 Rnds: Knit around.

THUMB GUSSET
Rnd 1: K3, place Color B marker, M1R, K1, M1L, place Color B marker, knit around: {26-30-34}{38-42-46} sts.

Rnd 2: Knit around, slipping Color B markers.

Rnd 3 (Increase rnd): Knit across to first Color B marker, slip marker, M1R, knit across to next Color B marker, M1L, slip marker, knit around: {28-32-36}{40-44-48} sts.

Repeat Rnds 2 and 3, {0-1-2}{3-4-4} time(s) *(see Zeros, page 40)*: {28-34-40}{46-52-56} sts.

Next Rnd: Knit across to CB marker, remove CB marker, thread yarn needle with waste yarn and slip the next {5-7-9}{11-13-13} sts **purlwise** onto the yarn needle, then onto the waste yarn to hold thumb sts, remove second CB marker, cast on one st using Backward Loop cast on *(Fig. 2, page 40)*, knit remaining sts: {24-28-32}{36-40-44} sts.

HAND

Knit every round until Mitten measures approximately {6¾-7-7¾}{8-9-9¾}"/ {17-18-19.5}{20.5-23-25} cm from cast on edge of Cuff **or** {1¼-1½-1¾}{2¼-2½-2¾}"/ {3-4-4.5}{5.5-6.5-7} cm less than desired finished length.

Fingertip Shaping

Rnd 1: K{4-5-6}{7-8-9}, K2 tog, ★ place Color B marker, K{4-5-6}{7-8-9}, K2 tog; repeat from ★ around: {20-24-28}{32-36-40} sts.

Rnd 2: Knit around, slipping Color B markers.

Rnd 3 (Decrease rnd)**:** ★ Knit across to within 2 sts of next Color B marker, K2 tog, slip marker; repeat from ★ 2 times **more**, knit across to within 2 sts of Color A marker, K2 tog: {16-20-24}{28-32-36} sts.

Repeat Rnds 2 and 3, {2-3-4}{5-6-7} times: 8 sts.

Cut yarn, leaving a long end for sewing.

Thread the yarn needle with the long end. Slip the remaining sts onto the yarn needle, then onto the long end; gather **tightly** to close the opening, then secure the end.

THUMB

Transfer first {2-3-4}{5-5-5} sts from waste yarn onto Needle 1, the next {2-3-4}{5-5-5} sts onto Needle 2, and the last {1-1-1}{1-3-3} st(s) onto Needle 3.

With **right** side facing and using Needle 3, pick up 4 sts from Hand to close the gap *(Fig.11a, page 43)*: {9-11-13}{15-17-17} sts.

Place Color A marker around the first stitch transferred to indicate the beginning of the round. Tie a scrap piece of yarn around the same stitch to aid in measuring the Thumb.

Knit every round until Thumb measures approximately {1¼-1¼-1½}{1¾-2-2}"/ {3-3-4}{4.5-5-5} cm from scrap yarn **or** ½" (1.5 cm) less than desired finished length.

Thumb Shaping

Rnd 1: K1, K2 tog around: {5-6-7}{8-9-9} sts.

Rnd 2: Knit around.

Rnd 3: K{1-0-1}{0-1-1}, K2 tog around: {3-3-4}{4-5-5} sts.

Cut yarn, leaving a long end for sewing.

Thread the yarn needle with the long end. Slip the remaining sts onto the yarn needle, then onto the long end; gather **tightly** to close the opening and secure the end.

LEFT MITTEN
CUFF

Work same as Right Mitten to Thumb Gusset, page 31: {24-28-32}{36-40-44} sts.

THUMB GUSSET

Rnd 1: Knit around to last 4 sts, place Color B marker, M1R, K1, M1L, place Color B marker, K3: {26-30-34}{38-42-46} sts.

Complete same as Right Mitten.

MULTI-CABLED BAG

Your friends will think you worked hard to make this cable-rich purse, but you will know that each cable is only four stitches wide. To assemble the body of the purse, you just pick up stitches on the side and bottom panels. The removable insert (see Finishing on page 38) is optional, but it is quick to sew and gives the purse a nice shape and additional sturdiness. Why not take the time to learn an easy cable and reward yourself with a big, beautiful bag you'll want to take everywhere?

Shown on page 35.

◼◼◼◻ **INTERMEDIATE**

Finished Measurements:
  14" (35.5 cm) square (at base) by 9" (23 cm) tall

MATERIALS
MEDIUM **④**
  Medium Weight Yarn
  [3.5 ounces, 155 yards
  (100 grams, 142 meters) per skein]:
    4 skeins
  Straight knitting needles, size 7 (4.5 mm) **or**
    size needed for gauge
  Cable needle
  Sheet of plastic canvas cut to 13" (33 cm) square
    for bottom
  ³/₄ yard (.69 meters) Quilted fabric
  8" (20.5 cm) diameter Circular purse handles
    (we used bamboo) - 2
  Markers - 14 (any color) and 4 split-ring
  Sewing needle and matching thread
  Yarn needle

GAUGE: In Stockinette Stitch
         (knit one row, purl one row),
         20 sts and 26 rows = 4" (10 cm)
         In Garter Stitch (knit every row),
         20 sts and 29 rows = 4" (10 cm)

Technique used:
P2 tog *(Fig. 7, page 42)*

STITCH GUIDE
Cables are achieved with a simple twisting, by exchanging the position of your stitches. The most common cables are formed by slipping part of the cable stitches "on-hold" onto a cable needle, then holding the stitches either in the "front" or in the "back" of your work. Stitches are worked from the left needle, then you work the "on-hold" stitches, either by working them directly from the cable needle **or** by slipping them back onto the left needle and working them.

CABLE 4 BACK *(abbreviated C4B)*
With yarn at the **back** of work, slip the next 2 sts purlwise onto the cable needle. Holding the cable needle at the **back** of work, knit the next 2 sts on the left needle, then knit the 2 sts on the cable needle *(Figs. 1a-d, page 2)*.
MAKE ONE PURL *(abbreviated M1P)*
With yarn at the **front** of work, insert the left needle under the horizontal strand between the stitches from the **back** *(Fig. 6a, page 42)*; then purl into the **front** of the strand.

PURSE
FIRST HANDLE CASING
Cast on 36 sts.

Row 1: Knit across.

Repeat Row 1 (Garter Stitch) until First Handle Casing measures approximately 4" (10 cm) from cast on edge.

BODY INCREASES
Row 1 (Right side)**:** P1, M1P, P2, place marker, (P1, K4, P1, place marker) 5 times, P2, M1P, P1: 38 sts.

Row 2: K4, slip next marker, (K1, P4, K1, slip next marker) 5 times, K4.

Row 3 (Increase row)**:** P1, M1P, P3, slip next marker, (P1, K4, P1, slip next marker) across to last 4 sts, P3, M1P, P1: 40 sts.

Row 4: K5, slip next marker, (K1, P4, K1, slip next marker) across to last 5 sts, K5.

Row 5 (Increase row - Cable row)**:** P1, M1P, P4, slip next marker, (P1, C4B, P1, slip next marker) across to last 5 sts, P4, M1P, P1: 42 sts.

Row 6: K6, slip next marker, (K1, P4, K1, slip next marker) across to last 6 sts, K6.

Row 7 (Increase row)**:** P1, place marker, M1P, K4, P1, slip next marker, (P1, K4, P1, slip next marker) across to last 6 sts, P1, K4, M1P, place marker, P1: 44 sts.

Row 8: K1, slip next marker, (K1, P4, K1, slip next marker) across to last st, K1.

Row 9 (Increase row)**:** P1, M1P, slip next marker, (P1, K4, P1, slip next marker) across to last st, M1P, P1: 46 sts.

Row 10: K2, slip next marker, (K1, P4, K1, slip next marker) across to last 2 sts, K2.

Row 11 (Increase row - Cable row)**:** P1, M1P, P1, slip next marker, (P1, C4B, P1, slip next marker) across to last 2 sts, P1, M1P, P1: 48 sts.

Row 12: K3, slip next marker, (K1, P4, K1, slip next marker) across to last 3 sts, K3.

Row 13 (Increase row)**:** P1, M1P, P2, slip next marker, (P1, K4, P1, slip next marker) across to last 3 sts, P2, M1P, P1: 50 sts.

Row 14: K4, slip next marker, (K1, P4, K1, slip next marker) across to last 4 sts, K4.

Rows 15-54: Repeat Rows 3-14, 3 times; then repeat Rows 3-6 once **more**: 90 sts.

BOTTOM PANEL
Row 1 (Right side)**:** P6, slip next marker, (P1, K4, P1, slip next marker) 13 times, P6.

Place a split-ring marker around the first and the last stitch on Row 1 to indicate the beginning of the Bottom Panel *(see Markers, page 40)*.

Row 2: K6, slip next marker, (K1, P4, K1, slip next marker) 13 times, K6.

Row 3: P6, slip next marker, (P1, K4, P1, slip next marker) 13 times, P6.

Row 4: K6, slip next marker, (K1, P4, K1, slip next marker) 13 times, K6.

Row 5 (Cable row): P6, slip next marker, (P1, C4B, P1, slip next marker) 13 times, P6.

Row 6: K6, slip next marker, (K1, P4, K1, slip next marker) 13 times, K6.

Row 7: P6, slip next marker, (P1, K4, P1, slip next marker) 13 times, P6.

Repeat Rows 2-7 until Bottom Panel measures approximately 14" (35.5 cm) from split-ring markers, ending by working Row 6.

Place a split-ring marker around the first and the last stitch of last row to indicate the end of the Bottom Panel.

BODY DECREASES

Row 1 (Decrease row): P1, P2 tog, P3, slip next marker, (P1, K4, P1, slip next marker) across to last 6 sts, P3, P2 tog, P1: 88 sts.

Row 2: K5, slip next marker, (K1, P4, K1, slip next marker) across to last 5 sts, K5.

Row 3 (Decrease row): P1, P2 tog, P2, slip next marker, (P1, K4, P1, slip next marker) across to last 5 sts, P2, P2 tog, P1: 86 sts.

Row 4: K4, slip next marker, (K1, P4, K1, slip next marker) across to last 4 sts, K4.

Row 5 (Decrease row - Cable row): P1, P2 tog, P1, slip next marker, (P1, C4B, P1, slip next marker) across to last 4 sts, P1, P2 tog, P1: 84 sts.

Row 6: K3, slip next marker, (K1, P4, K1, slip next marker) across to last 3 sts, K3.

Row 7 (Decrease row): P1, P2 tog, slip next marker, (P1, K4, P1, slip next marker) across to last 3 sts, P2 tog, P1: 82 sts.

Row 8: K2, slip next marker, (K1, P4, K1, slip next marker) across to last 2 sts, K2.

Row 9 (Decrease row): P1, slip next st **purlwise** from **left** needle to **right** needle, remove next marker, return slipped st **back** onto left needle, P2 tog, P5, slip next marker, (P1, K4, P1, slip next marker) across to last 8 sts, P5, slip next st **purlwise** from **left** needle to **right** needle, remove next marker, return slipped st **back** onto left needle, P2 tog, P1: 80 sts.

Row 10: K7, slip next marker, (K1, P4, K1, slip next marker) across to last 7 sts, K7.

Row 11 (Decrease row - Cable row): P1, P2 tog, P4, slip next marker, (P1, C4B, P1, slip next marker) across to last 7 sts, P4, P2 tog, P1: 78 sts.

Row 12: K6, slip next marker, (K1, P4, K1, slip next marker) across to last 6 sts, K6.

Rows 13-54: Repeat Rows 1-12, 3 times; then repeat Rows 1-6 once **more**: 36 sts.

Row 55: P3, slip next marker, (P1, K4, P1, slip next marker) 5 times, P3.

Row 56: Knit across, removing markers from needle.

SECOND HANDLE CASING
Row 1: Knit across.

Repeat Row 1 (Garter Stitch) until Second Handle Casing measures approximately 4" (10 cm), ending by working a **wrong** side row.

Bind off remaining sts in **knit**.

SIDE PANEL 1
With **right** side of Bottom Panel facing, pick up 84 sts evenly spaced across end of rows from the first split-ring marker to the second split-ring marker *(Fig. 11b, page 43)*; do **not** remove split-ring markers.

Work in Garter Stitch for 3 rows.

Row 1 (Right side): P3, place marker, (P1, K4, P1, place marker) 13 times, P3.

Row 2: K3, slip next marker, (K1, P4, K1, slip next marker) across to last 3 sts, K3.

Row 3: P3, slip next marker, (P1, K4, P1, slip next marker) across to last 3 sts, P3.

Row 4: K3, slip next marker, (K1, P4, K1, slip next marker) across to last 3 sts, K3.

Row 5 (Cable row): P3, slip next marker, (P1, C4B, P1, slip next marker) across to last 3 sts, P3.

Rows 6-56: Repeat Rows 6-56 of Body Decreases: 36 sts.

Row 57: Purl across.

Row 58: Knit across.

Row 59: Purl across.

Bind off remaining sts in **knit**.

SIDE PANEL 2
With **right** side of opposite side of Bottom Panel facing, pick up 84 sts evenly spaced across end of rows from the first split-ring marker to the second split-ring marker; do **not** remove split-ring markers.

Work in Garter Stitch for 3 rows.

Row 1 (Right side): P3, place marker, (P1, K4, P1, place marker) 13 times, P3.

Row 2: K3, slip next marker, (K1, P4, K1, slip next marker) across to last 3 sts, K3.

Row 3: P3, slip next marker, (P1, K4, P1, slip next marker) across to last 3 sts, P3.

Row 4: K3, slip next marker, (K1, P4, K1, slip next marker) across to last 3 sts, K3.

Row 5 (Cable row): P3, slip next marker, (P1, C4B, P1, slip next marker) across to last 3 sts, P3.

Rows 6-56: Repeat Rows 6-56 of Body Decreases, page 36: 36 sts.

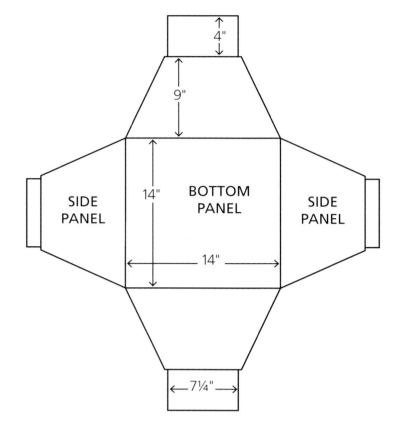

Row 57: Purl across.

Row 58: Knit across.

Row 59: Purl across.

Bind off remaining sts in **knit**.

Keep split-ring markers at the corners of the Bottom Panel for seaming reference. Wash according to yarn label. Block to schematic measurements *(see Blocking, page 43)*. Let air dry.

FINISHING

Fold sides up using the split-ring markers as the four corners of the purse. With **right** side facing, leaving top 3 rows unsewn on each Side Panel and letting the fabric roll toward the center opening of the purse, weave seams *(Fig. 12, page 43)*.

Place one Purse Handle at center of either Handle Casing. Sew top edge of Handle Casing to bottom edge of Handle Casing.

Repeat with second Handle on opposite Handle Casing.

Cut quilted fabric to 14" x 30" (35.5 x 76 cm). With **right** side together, fold piece in half having short edges together and sew both side edges, using a ¹/₂" (12 mm) seam allowance. Turn right side out. Slide plastic canvas into fabric envelope. Fold open raw edges to wrong side of fabric and stitch opening closed. Place in bottom of purse.

GENERAL INSTRUCTIONS

ABBREVIATIONS

C4B	Cable 4 Back
C5B	Cable 5 Back
C8B	Cable 8 Back
C10B	Cable 10 Back
C10F	Cable 10 Front
cm	centimeters
K	knit
M1L	Make One Left
M1P	Make One Purl
M1R	Make One Right
mm	millimeters
P	purl
Rnd(s)	Round(s)
SSK	slip, slip, knit
st(s)	stitch(es)
tog	together
YO	yarn over

SYMBOLS & TERMS

★ — work instructions following ★ as many **more** times as indicated in addition to the first time.

( ) or [ ] — work enclosed instructions **as many** times as specified by the number immediately following **or** contains explanatory remarks.

colon (:) — the numbers given after a colon at the end of a row or round denotes the number of stitches you should have on that row or round.

KNIT TERMINOLOGY	
UNITED STATES	**INTERNATIONAL**
gauge =	tension
bind off =	cast off
yarn over (YO) =	yarn forward (yfwd) **or** yarn around needle (yrn)

Yarn Weight Symbol & Names	LACE 0	SUPER FINE 1	FINE 2	LIGHT 3	MEDIUM 4	BULKY 5	SUPER BULKY 6
Type of Yarns in Category	Fingering, size 10 crochet thread	Sock, Fingering, Baby	Sport, Baby	DK, Light Worsted	Worsted, Afghan, Aran	Chunky, Craft, Rug	Bulky, Roving
Knit Gauge Range* in Stockinette St to 4" (10 cm)	33-40** sts	27-32 sts	23-26 sts	21-24 sts	16-20 sts	12-15 sts	6-11 sts
Advised Needle Size Range	000-1	1 to 3	3 to 5	5 to 7	7 to 9	9 to 11	11 and larger

*GUIDELINES ONLY: The chart above reflects the most commonly used gauges and needle sizes for specific yarn categories.

** Lace weight yarns are usually knitted on larger needles to create lacy openwork patterns. Accordingly, a gauge range is difficult to determine. Always follow the gauge stated in your pattern.

GAUGE

Exact gauge is **essential** for proper size. Before beginning your project, make a sample swatch in the yarn and needle specified in the individual instructions. After completing the swatch, measure it, counting your stitches and rows or rounds carefully. If your swatch is larger or smaller than specified, **make another, changing needle size to get the correct gauge.** Keep trying until you find the size needles that will give you the specified gauge. Once proper gauge is obtained, measure width of piece approximately every 3" (7.5 cm) to be sure gauge remains consistent.

ZEROS

To consolidate the length of an involved pattern, zeros are sometimes used so that all sizes can be combined. For example, P1{0-1-0} means that the first and third sizes would P1, and the second and fourth sizes would do nothing.

MARKERS

As a convenience to you, we have used markers to mark the beginning of a round or to mark the beginning of each pattern repeat. Place markers as instructed. You may use purchased markers or tie a length of contrasting color yarn around the needle. When you reach a marker, slip it from the left needle to the right needle; remove it when no longer needed.

When using double-pointed needles, a split-ring marker can be placed around the first stitch in the round to indicate the beginning of the round. Move it up at the end of each round.

BACKWARD LOOP CAST ON

Make a backward loop with the working yarn and place it on the needle *(Fig. 2)*.

Fig. 2

KNITTING NEEDLES																
U.S.	0	1	2	3	4	5	6	7	8	9	10	10½	11	13	15	17
U.K.	13	12	11	10	9	8	7	6	5	4	3	2	1	00	000	---
Metric - mm	2	2.25	2.75	3.25	3.5	3.75	4	4.5	5	5.5	6	6.5	8	9	10	12.75

◖□□□ **BEGINNER**	Projects for first-time knitters using basic knit and purl stitches. Minimal shaping.
◖■□□ **EASY**	Projects using basic stitches, repetitive stitch patterns, simple color changes, and simple shaping and finishing.
◖■■□ **INTERMEDIATE**	Projects with a variety of stitches, such as basic cables and lace, simple intarsia, double-pointed needles and knitting in the round needle techniques, mid-level shaping and finishing.
◖■■◗ **EXPERIENCED**	Projects using advanced techniques and stitches, such as short rows, fair isle, more intricate intarsia, cables, lace patterns, and numerous color changes.

CIRCULAR KNITTING

Circular knitting is working around and around the needle(s) in a continuous spiral to create a seamless piece such as a hat or mittens.

The **right** side of the piece is always facing you as you work around the outside of the circle, and is usually knit using a circular knitting needle **or** a set of 4 double-pointed knitting needles, depending on the number of stitches being worked.

USING A CIRCULAR NEEDLE

Cast on as many stitches as instructed. Untwist and straighten the stitches on the needle to be sure that the cast on ridge lies on the inside of the needle and never rolls around the needle *(Fig. 3)*. Hold the needle so that the ball of yarn is attached to the stitch closest to the right-hand point. Place a marker on the right-hand point to mark the beginning of the rounds *(see Markers, page 40)*. Work across the stitches on the left-hand point.

Check to be sure that the cast on edge has not twisted around the needle. If it has, it is impossible to untwist it. The only way to fix this is to rip it out and return to the cast on row.

Fig. 3

USING DOUBLE-POINTED NEEDLES

Cast on as many stitches as instructed. Slipping the stitches **purlwise**, divide the stitches evenly between three double-pointed needles *(Fig. 4a)*. Form a triangle with the needles, having the ball of yarn that is attached to the third needle at the top right and making sure that the stitches are not twisted, with the cast on ridge lying to the inside of the triangle.

With the remaining needle, work across the stitches on the first needle *(Fig. 4b)*, placing a split-ring marker around the first stitch worked to mark the beginning of the round *(see Markers, page 40)*. You will now have an empty needle with which to work the stitches from the next needle. Work the first stitch of each needle firmly to prevent gaps. Continue working around without turning the work.

Fig. 4a

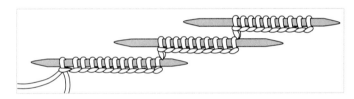

Fig. 4b

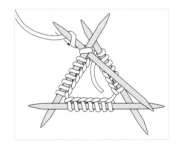

INCREASES

MAKE ONE LEFT *(abbreviated M1L)*

Insert the left needle under the horizontal strand between the stitches from the **front** *(Fig. 5a)*, then knit into the **back** of the strand *(Fig. 5b)*.

Fig. 5a

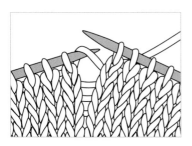

Fig. 5b

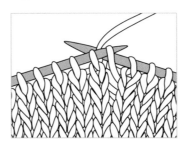

MAKE ONE RIGHT *(abbreviated M1R)*

Insert the left needle under the horizontal strand between the stitches from the **back** *(Fig. 6a)*, then knit into the **front** of the strand *(Fig. 6b)*.

Fig. 6a

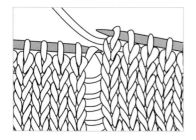

Fig. 6b

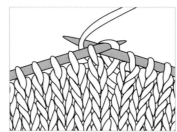

DECREASES

KNIT 2 TOGETHER *(abbreviated K2 tog)*

Insert the right needle into the **front** of the first two stitches on the left needle as if to **knit** *(Fig. 7)*, then knit them together as if they were one stitch.

Fig. 7

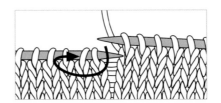

PURL 2 TOGETHER *(abbreviated P2 tog)*

Insert the right needle into the **front** of the first two stitches on the left needle as if to **purl** *(Fig. 8)*, then **purl** them together as if they were one stitch.

Fig. 8

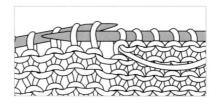

SLIP, SLIP, KNIT *(abbreviated SSK)*

Slip the first stitch as if to knit, then slip the next stitch as if to knit *(Fig. 9a)*. Insert the left needle into the front of both slipped stitches *(Fig. 9b)* and knit them together as if they were one stitch *(Fig. 9c)*.

Fig. 9a

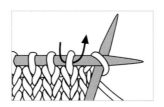

Fig. 9b

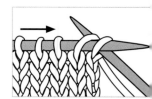

Fig. 9c

YARN OVERS *(abbreviated YO)*

A yarn over is simply placing the yarn over the right needle creating an extra stitch. Since the yarn over does produce a hole in the knit fabric, it is used for a lacy effect. On the row following a yarn over, you must be careful to keep it on the needle and treat it as a stitch by knitting or purling it as instructed.

Bring the yarn forward **between** the needles, then back over the top of the right-hand needle, so that it is now in position to knit the next stitch *(Fig. 10)*.

Fig. 10

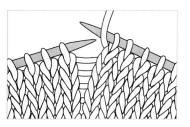

PICKING UP STITCHES

When instructed to pick up stitches, insert the needle from the **front** to the **back** under two strands at the edge of the worked piece. Put the yarn around the needle as if to **knit**, then bring the needle with the yarn back through the stitch to the right side, resulting in a stitch on the needle *(Figs. 11a & b)*.

Fig. 11a   Fig. 11b

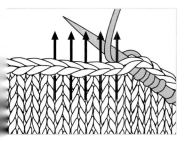   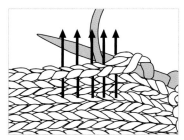

WEAVING SEAMS

With the **right** side of both pieces facing you and edges even, sew through both pieces once to secure the beginning of the seam, leaving an ample yarn end to weave in later. Insert the needle under the bar **between** the first and second stitches on the row and pull the yarn through *(Fig. 12)*. Insert the needle under the next bar on the second side. Repeat from side to side, being careful to match rows. If the edges are different lengths, it may be necessary to insert the needle under two bars at one edge.

Fig. 12

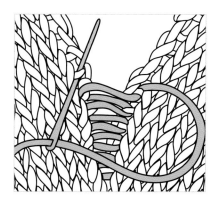

BLOCKING

Check the yarn label for any special instructions about blocking. With acrylics that can be blocked, place your project on a clean terry towel over a flat surface and pin in place to the desired size using rust-proof pins where needed. Cover it with dampened bath towels. When the towels are dry, the project is blocked.

Another method of blocking that is especially good for wool requires the use of a steam iron or a handheld steamer. Place your project on a clean terry towel over a flat surface and shape to size; pin in place using rust-proof pins where needed. Hold a steam iron or steamer just above the item and steam it thoroughly. Never let the weight of the iron touch the item because it will flatten the stitches. Leave the item pinned until it is completely dry.

BASIC SKILLS

SLINGSHOT CAST ON

Step 1: Pull a length of yarn from the skein, allowing approximately 1" (2.5 cm) of yarn for each stitch to be cast on. Make a slip knot at the measured distance, pulling gently on both yarn ends to tighten stitch on needle.

Step 2: Hold the needle in your right hand with your index finger resting on the slip knot.

Step 3: Place the short end of the yarn over your left thumb, and bring the working yarn up and over you left index finger. Hold both yarn ends in your left palm with your 3 remaining fingers *(Fig. 13a)*.

Fig. 13a

Step 4: Insert the tip of the needle **under** the first strand of yarn on your left thumb *(Fig. 13b)*.

Fig. 13b

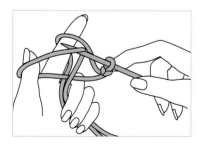

Step 5: Bring the needle **over** and around the first strand on your index finger *(Fig. 13c)*.

Fig. 13c

Step 6: Pull the yarn and needle down through the loop on your thumb *(Fig. 13d)*.

Fig. 13d

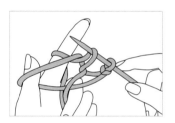

Step 7: Slip your thumb out of the loop and bring it toward you, catching the yarn end to form a new loop on your thumb *(Fig. 13e)*, and gently pulling to tighten the new stitch on the needle. Rest your index finger on the new stitch.

Fig. 13e

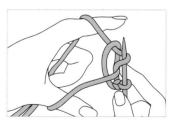

Repeat Steps 4-7 for each additional stitch.

KNIT STITCH *(abbreviated K)*
ENGLISH METHOD

Step 1: Hold the needle with the stitches in your left hand and the empty needle in your right hand.

Step 2: With the working yarn in **back** of the needles, insert the right needle into the stitch closest to the tip of the left needle as shown in **Fig. 14a**.

Fig. 14a

Step 3: Hold the right needle with your left thumb and index finger while you bring the yarn beneath the right needle and between the needles from **back** to **front** *(Fig. 14b)*.

Fig. 14b

Step 4: With your right hand, bring the right needle (with the loop of yarn) toward you and through the stitch *(Figs. 14c & d)*. Slip the old stitch off the left needle and gently pull to tighten the new stitch on the shaft of the right needle.

Fig. 14c

Fig. 14d

CONTINENTIAL METHOD

Step 1: Hold the needle with the stitches in your left hand and the empty needle in your right hand. Loop the working yarn over the index finger of your left hand and hold it loosely across the palm of your hand with your little finger.

Step 2: With the yarn in **back** of the needles, insert the right needle into the stitch closest to the tip of the left needle as shown in **Fig. 15a**.

Fig. 15a

Step 3: With your left index finger, bring the yarn between the needles from **left** to **right** around the needle *(Fig. 15b)*.

Fig. 15b

Step 4: With your right hand, bring the right needle (with the loop of yarn) toward you and through the stitch *(Figs. 15c & d)*. Slip the old stitch off the left needle and gently pull to tighten the new stitch on the shaft of the right needle.

Fig. 15c

Fig. 15d

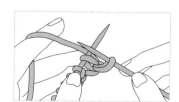

PURL STITCH *(abbreviated P)*
ENGLISH METHOD

Step 1: Hold the needle with the stitches in your left hand and the empty needle in your right hand.

Step 2: With the yarn in **front** of the needles, insert the right needle into the front of the stitch as shown in **Fig. 16a**.

Fig. 16a

Step 3: Hold the right needle with your left thumb and index finger while you bring the yarn between the needles from **right to left** and around the right needle *(Fig. 16b)*.

Fig. 16b

Step 4: Move the right needle (with the loop of yarn) through the stitch and away from you *(Fig. 16c)*. Slip the old stitch off the left needle and gently pull to tighten the new stitch on the shaft of the right needle.

Fig. 16c

CONTINENTAL METHOD

Step 1: Hold the needle with the stitches in your left hand and the empty needle in your right hand. Loop the working yarn over the index finger of your left hand and hold it loosely across the palm of your hand with your little finger.

Step 2: With the yarn in **front** of the needles, insert the right needle into the front of the stitch as shown in **Fig. 17a**.

Fig. 17a

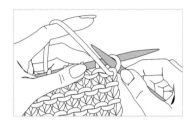

Step 3: With your left index finger, bring the yarn between the needles from **right to left** around the right needle *(Fig. 17b)*.

Fig. 17b

Step 4: Move your left index finger forward while moving the right needle (with the loop of yarn) through the stitch and away from you *(Fig. 17c)*. Slip the old stitch off the left needle and gently pull to tighten the new stitch on the shaft of the right needle.

Fig. 17c

BIND OFF

Binding off is the method used to remove and secure your stitches from the knitting needles so that they don't unravel.

Work the first two stitches.

Use your left needle as a tool to lift the second stitch on the right needle up and over the first stitch *(Fig. 18a)* and completely off the right needle *(Fig. 18b)*. Don't forget to remove the left needle from the stitch.

Fig. 18a

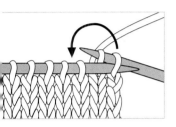

Fig. 18b

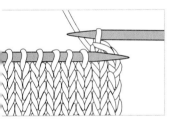

You now have one stitch on your right needle and you have bound off one stitch. Count the stitch as you bind it off, not as you work it.

Work the next stitch; you will have two stitches on the right needle. Bind off as before.

Continue until your left needle is empty and there is only one stitch left on your right needle.

Cut the yarn, leaving a long end to hide later.

Slip the stitch off the right needle; pull the end through the stitch *(Fig. 18c)* and tighten the stitch.

Fig. 18c

BASIC CABLES

Cables are achieved with a simple twisting, by exchanging the position of your stitches. The most common cables are formed by slipping part of the cable stitches "on-hold" onto a cable needle, then holding the stitches either in the "front" or in the "back" of your work. Stitches are worked from the left needle, then you work the "on-hold" stitches, either by working them directly from the cable needle **or** by slipping them back onto the left needle and working them *(Figs. 1a-d, page 2)*.

YARN INFORMATION

The projects in this leaflet were made using a variety of yarns. Any brand in the specified weight may be used. It is best to refer to the yardage/meters when determining how many balls, skeins, or hanks to purchase. Remember, to arrive at the finished size, it is the GAUGE/TENSION that is important, not the brand of yarn.

For your convenience, listed below are the specific yarns used to create our photography models.

STARTER CABLE SCARF & HAT
Lion Brand® Wool-Ease® Chunky
#135 Spice

IMPRESSIVE SCARF & HAT
Lion Brand® Wool-Ease® Thick & Quick®
#099 Fisherman

LUCKY HORSESHOE HAND WARMERS
Cascade Yarns® Heritage Sock Yarn
#5607

KEYHOLE SCARF & COZY MITTENS
Bernat® Roving
#00011 Bark

THREE-CABLE HAND WARMERS
Stitch Nation by Debbie Stoller™ Alpaca Love™
#3810 Lake

LONG SPIRAL SCARF & SIMPLE HAT
Cascade Yarns® Di.Ve' Autunno
#25741

COLOR-CHANGING SCARF
Cascade Yarns® Cascade 220
Light Color - #2440 Vinci
Medium Color - #9537 Cedar Tweed
Dark Color - #9408 Cordovan

THREE-PIECE GIFT SET
Patons® SWS
#70117 Natural Denim

MULTI-CABLED BAG
Stitch Nation by Debbie Stoller™ Full O' Sheep™
#2630 Meadow

CLASSIC RIBBED SCARF & HAT
Cascade Yarns® Pastaza
#073

PRODUCTION TEAM-
Writer/Technical Editor: Linda A. Daley
Editorial Writer: Susan McManus Johnson
Senior Graphic Artist: Shibaguyz Designz, Jason Mullett-Bowlsby Project Manager
Photo Stylist: Brook Duszota
Photographer: Jason Masters